The Truth Se

No One Loves As He Loves!

Roger Henri Trepanier

© 2015

This book is dedicated to all the men, women, and children of this world who by God's grace have come to experience the love of God centered in the cross:

"We know love by this, that He laid down His life for us…"

1 John 3:16 in part

**Titles available from Roger Henri Trepanier in
The Truth Seeker's Library™ series:**

God Did Not Create Human Beings To Die… But To Live On…
Eternally!
Finding Comfort And Encouragement In The Promises Of God In The
Last Days
How We Know For Sure That We Are Living In The Last Days!
Have You Ever Wondered What Happens After Death?
An Introduction To The New World That Is Coming On The Earth
Deeper Truths Of The Christian Life
Evangelism As God Intended
Keeping On Serving God In The Last Days
The Mysterious World Of Angels And Demons

**Titles available from Roger Henri Trepanier in
The Practical Helps Library™ series:**

Learning to Overcome The Perplexities Of This Present Life
So, I Hear You Want To Work With Seniors?
I Will Not Have This Man To Rule Over Me!
Spiritual Truth To Warm The Heart!

**Other titles available from Roger Henri Trepanier
in The Christian Fiction Library™ series:**

The Beginning Of A New Dawn
It Is Never Too Late For Love!
The True To Life Musings Of Fred And Ernie
Between A Rock And A Hard Place!

INTRODUCTION

One thing I have discovered in my over six decades of living is that people are starved for love! But that does not include all the different kinds of love. What I mean is that there is no lack for a certain kind of love, which is the love of money! But when it comes to the love to be seen among human beings, there is a great lack of that love. And there is an even greater lack for another kind of love, which is love for God by human beings. However, what is absolutely sure is that there is a love that never varies and is constant at all times, which is the love which God has for human beings. There are no bounds to that love. And this is the love we will mostly be concentrating on in this book.

What led me to write this book is that two weeks ago God once again displayed just how much He loved His servant, even though I am totally undeserving of that love. In other words, I realized once again that this kind of love, namely the love God has and displays toward human beings, is supernatural, in that it not only originates with God, but it loves what from a human standpoint is unlovable. To get a handle on this here, please consider that we find it fairly easy to love those who love us, but how about when it comes to loving someone who we find repugnant, in terms of someone who turns us off, either when we look at them, or in their behavior, in what they say and do. That is a different story altogether. To love people that we find unlovable requires a love that is beyond our capacity to produce.

But what is also true is that we even have difficulty loving God, even though He is not unlovable, like some people tend to be. And it is not just because we do not see God that we find it hard to love Him, although that is certainly a factor. One reason for our difficulty in loving God is that we often do not know how. In other words, we have to learn how to love God, which is learned from God directly in His word. That is, God Himself teaches us how to love Him in His word, the Bible. But then this book is not about our loving God, but rather it has its focus on God's love for us, in terms of considering just how much God loves us. Sometimes we may see a man and woman together who are in love, with the woman saying to the man, "Do you love me?," with the man then replying, "Let me count the ways!" Well, that is what we will be doing in this book; we will count the ways, chapter by chapter, of just how much God loves us!

What should also be mentioned before closing this Introduction is that after completing 21 years of formal education and then spending almost 28 years working in Project Engineering and management in the Corporate offices of a large utility, God called His servant as a non-denominational evangelist in early 1999, then sent him out over 3000 miles, away from family and friends, to the place of service God assigned; where His servant has been and is still serving Him as evangelist, counselor, author, editor, and publisher. The author is a widower with three adopted children, now married.

A website has been established for the purpose of interacting with readers, which can be found at:

http://www.pilgrimpathwaypublications.com

God also led His servant to establish another website specifically for gospel ministry, since the author is an evangelist. That website can be found at:

http://www.servantofmosthigh.com

And now my prayer is that God will richly bless you as you read this book and greatly minister to your every need in your life, as only God can! To Him be all praise, honor, and glory, with thanksgiving, both now and forevermore! Amen.

CONTENTS

                                                        Page

Introduction

Chapter One   God's love for human beings has a
                     beginning in time and a purpose 11

Chapter Two   God's love for human beings
                     involves a total giving of Himself 15

Chapter Three   God's love for human beings made
                     the forgiveness of sins available to
                     all 25

Chapter Four   God's love for human beings made
                     eternal life available to all 31

Chapter Five   God's love is to be seen as always
                     being in and through His Son 35

Chapter Six   God's love is to be the basis for our
                     loving other human beings 39

Chapter Seven   God's love is to be the basis for
                     keeping a marriage relationship
                     going 43

Chapter Eight   God's love is to be the basis for our
                     service to God 47

Chapter Nine   God's love is the basis for our
                     worship of God 51

Chapter Ten   God's love is to be seen as a gift
                     we do not deserve 55

Chapter Eleven   God's love is to be seen as being
                     unconditional 61

Chapter Twelve   God's love is the basis for our
                     sense of security and peace while
                     on earth 67

Chapter Thirteen   God's love means we have a
                         shoulder to cry on and a place to
                         lay our burdens 73

Chapter Fourteen   God's love is given to be shared
                         with others 77

Chapter Fifteen   Seeing God's promises as being
                         secret love notes which He sends
                         to His own! 81

Chapter Sixteen   When we come in contact with
                         God's love, we come in contact with
                         God Himself! 87

Chapter Seventeen   A last word 91

Addendum   For those who may not as yet know
                         God 97

The Next Book   103

The first words God ever spoke are at Genesis 1:1, "In the beginning God created the heavens and the earth." How often do we consider that God created this earth in order to have a place to display the full extent of His love for the human beings He was to place on this earth?

CHAPTER ONE

/ God's love for human beings has a beginning in time and a purpose

Before creation took place and time began, God's love was already in existence and was being displayed among the three Persons of Father, Son, and Holy Spirit making up our One God. However, even though God is eternally existing, it was never His intention to keep His love only within Himself. In other words, He wanted to have people to display His love to. We will get the idea here if we consider for a moment what often happens after a man and woman marry. What brings them together in the first place is a deep mutual love for each other, which says, "I want you only above any other and I want to spend the rest of my life with you." It is that kind of love which God intends and which leads to marriage, to sexual intimacy in marriage, and then to offspring as a result of that sexual intimacy in marriage. In other words, the offspring are the result of the love a husband and wife have for each other. The same is true, but to a much higher degree, for the love God has for us as human beings. The love that the three Persons of our One God had for each other led to the creation of man, so that God would have offspring to show forth His love to!

Did you ever consider that one purpose God had for putting human beings on this earth was to display the full extent of His love to us? Mind boggling, if you ask me, but nevertheless true! God's love, which is part of the makeup of our eternal God, was meant to be shared; it was never meant to stand alone. In fact, when we come to be a recipient of God's love, we will find that we cannot keep it to ourselves, for it is a love which wants to give itself to others. It is not like the love of money that was mentioned in the Introduction, or even the love that we have for ourselves apart from God, which only has one object, which is me, myself, and I; and no one else. Therefore, let us remember that the love we have in view in this book is the love which has its origin in God, which He started to display outside of Himself at creation, and which was meant to be shared with others. Once we have this love in our lives, it will change us forever!

God does not just talk about love; He demonstrates what love is like through the love He continually displays!

CHAPTER TWO

/ God's love for human beings involves a total giving of Himself

When God loves, it is not as we love. He does not just love in half-measure, but His love is always a total giving of Himself, with nothing held back. And since there is only one God (1 Corinthians 8:6), who has made Himself known in three Persons as Father, Son, and Holy Spirit (Matthew 28:19), this further means that this One God made up of Three Persons is indivisible, so that for our present purpose this means that when God loves, it is a total giving of all three Persons that is involved with nothing held back. Before returning to this truth at the end of the chapter, let us first go on to look at the love which each Person of our Triune (Three in One) God has for human beings, as disclosed to us by God in His word.

The love of God The Father

And one place to begin looking at that display of God The Father's love is to note what God says in that familiar verse of God's word at John 3:16, "For God so loved the world, that He gave His only begotten Son, that whoever believes in Him shall not perish, but have eternal life." Anyone who thinks about this for a moment will realize that "the world" God has in view here is 'the people of this world.' In other words, the people inhabiting this earth in time, from Adam and Eve onwards, are who "God so loved." And how did God demonstrate His love for the people of the world? The answer is that "He gave His only begotten Son." That statement will not hit home to us until we realize that the 'giving' by God The Father of His precious Son here meant that He was giving His only and precious Son over to death for our sakes!

One would have to search far and wide in order to find parents who would be willing to give up one's child unto death. That is just not done among us, at least not in a society that had its beginning under The God of the Bible. But yet that is what God did when He gave His own precious Son unto death, out of love for the human race. But then God had a very good reason for doing so. Let us note what God says in His word at Isaiah 59:2, "But your iniquities have made a separation between you and your God, and your sins have hidden His face from you so that He does not hear." So we see that the reason that God took the drastic step of giving up His only Son unto death was because we, as a human race, had been separated from Him due to our sins against Him. In other words, what happened right at the beginning of creation is that our first set of parents, from whom we all come from, and who had been created by God as sinless, one day sinned against God and so brought the whole human race under the condemnation of death due to sin, noting what God says in His word at Romans 5:12, "Therefore, just as through one man (Adam) sin entered into the world, and death through sin, and so death spread to all men, because all sinned…"

We need to catch the importance of what God says here. Sin entered the world we live in here on earth because Adam and Eve sinned against God as representative of us all - in that if we had been in their place we would have sinned exactly as they did – and since the penalty for sin was death (Genesis 2:16,17 with Romans 6:23), then the whole human race not only inherits the sinful nature of our first parents at birth, but we also fall under the same condemnation they did, which is the penalty of death, when we sin at the moment of reaching the age of accountability, which is the moment in time known only to God when we as an infant come to realize right from wrong and choose the wrong, thereby becoming personally accountable to God for our sin.

And so it was because the whole human race fell under the condemnation of death due to sin that God gave His only begotten Son unto death. Then coming back to the first part of John 3:16 that we quoted above, we note that it was out of love for all human beings to be born in time that God gave His only begotten Son. When God The Father gave His only Son, He was giving all He had to give, holding nothing back! God had created human beings to display His love to, and now He had made the provision for the first display of that love through His own precious Son's death on behalf of the human race, which had become separated from Him due to sin.

The love of God's Son

And we are to see that God did not stop there, noting what He further discloses to us in His word at 1 John 3:16 regarding the love of The Son of God for human beings, "We know love by this, that He laid down His life for us; and we ought to lay down our lives for the brethren." Now it is The Son of God Who is here in view as having laid down His life out of love for all human beings, when He died in our place at the cross, bearing there the death that was due our sins. Let us note what God adds at 1 Peter 3:18 in part, "For Christ also died for sins once for all, the just for the unjust, so that He might bring us to God..." In saying "the just for the unjust" here, God is pointing out the fact that His Son had no sin and so did not deserve to die. He only died to provide His Father a basis by which to forgive the sins, and provide eternal life, for any human being who would believe in Him, as we see in the second part of John 3:16 quoted above, "that whoever believes in Him shall not perish, but have eternal life."

And so at John 3:16 we have seen the love of God The Father for the human race as a total giving of Himself, with nothing held back, when He gave His own precious Son unto death, to be the basis by which our sins could be forgiven and that we could then have eternal life with Him. But in order for that to happen, The Son of God had to fully and willingly give Himself unto death on our behalf, as our Substitute, as we see at 1 John 3:16. In other words, it also required a total giving of Himself, with nothing held back, as a demonstration of His love for human beings, or else His Father would have no basis by which to forgive the sins of human beings and to impart eternal life with Himself. That is why God can say at 1 John 3:16, "We (as human beings) know love by this, that He (God's only begotten Son, Jesus Christ) laid down His life for us," that is, for all sinners, which the whole of the human race becomes from the moment of the age of accountability onwards.

What needs to also be remembered here regarding the love of The Son of God is the truth that God's love has been ongoing from eternity past, even before creation took place and time began. In other words, God's love did not just begin when He gave His precious Son. And what we need to note at this point is what God tells us at Philippians 2:5-8 (being here a translation taken from both the NKJV and the NIV, as indicated), "[5] Let this mind be in you which was also in Christ Jesus (NKJV), [6] Who, being in very nature God, did not consider equality with God something to be grasped (NIV), [7] but made Himself of no reputation (NKJV), taking the very nature of a servant, being made in human likeness. [8] And being found in appearance as a man, He humbled Himself and became obedient to death - even death on a cross!" (NIV)

And so looking at the above passage from Philippians in a little greater detail, we see that what we are told here at verses 5 to 7 took place in Heaven before The Son of God took on the human body prepared by His Father in the womb of a woman who was a virgin, with verse 8 then having in view the birth and earthly life of God's precious Son, culminating in His death at the cross on our behalf. What this means is that we see The Son of God even in eternity past agreeing to be a servant unto His Father for the sake of our redemption during time, once God had created us and we had all gone into sin as a human race. What this further means for our present subject is that the love of The Son of God for the human race did not just begin when God's precious Son gave Himself over to death on a cross for us, but rather began in eternity past, when God's Son first gave Himself to His Father as a servant, for the sake of our redemption. And so even at Isaiah 42, a long time before the moment of His Incarnation, we see God's precious Son spoken of by God The Father as "My Servant."

The love of God's Holy Spirit

God talks of The Holy Spirit's involvement in the love of God at least twice in His word, noting what we read first at Romans 15:30, "Now I urge you, brethren, by our Lord Jesus Christ and by the love of the Spirit, to strive together with me in your prayers to God for me," and then also at Galatians 5:22, "But the fruit of the Spirit is love, joy, peace, patience, kindness, goodness, faithfulness..."

But this is not all, since God is made up of three indivisible Persons of Father, Son, and Holy Spirit, this further means that The Holy Spirit also needs to be seen as fully involved in the total giving of Himself as a demonstration of the love of God for human beings. And in order to grasp what is involved here, let us note two truths which

God shares with us in His word, the first being at Ephesians 1:13,14, where we read, "[13] In Him (in God's Son, Jesus Christ), you also, after listening to the message of truth, the gospel of your salvation — having also believed, you were sealed in Him with the Holy Spirit of promise, [14] who is given as a pledge of our inheritance, with a view to the redemption of God's own possession, to the praise of His glory." And so the first truth God shares here is that at the moment of believing the gospel - which is God's good news regarding His precious Son, Jesus Christ, namely that He died for our sins, that He was buried, and that He was raised from the dead the third day – then upon believing, God The Father gives one the forgiveness of sins and eternal life with Himself at the moment that He gives The Holy Spirit to indwell one's human spirit, as a deposit guaranteeing that one day, one who has so believed and received The Holy Spirit will indeed be in Heaven with God forever!

Then the second truth that God shares, which brings into focus the total giving love of The Holy Spirit for human beings, is found in what God says in His word at Ephesians 4:30, where we read, "Do not grieve the Holy Spirit of God, by whom you were sealed for the day of redemption." What we need to grasp here is that when The Holy Spirit comes to permanently indwell a believer at salvation, which is what the word "sealed" refers to here, that believer is initially cleansed of all past sins committed, from the age of accountability onwards. And although that is true, nevertheless a believer can still sin due to having a sinful nature, which will be with us until that day of redemption, which is when God comes to bring us to Heaven bodily at the end of the present age. But until then, The Holy Spirit is grieved over and over again every time we sin. What this means then is that The Holy Spirit had to love human beings with a total giving of Himself, holding nothing back, in order to be willing to come to indwell us, when He knew that He would be suffering over and over again each time a human being as now a believer sins!

Let us pause to think about this for a moment, of just how much our Holy God must suffer every time we sin, since God is One and is indivisible, which in reality means that it is God The Father Who indwells us through His Son by His Holy Spirit! And so we see here that our redemption required a total giving out of love for us of The Father, The Son, and The Holy Spirit. Therefore, as we go on, let us remember that God's love for human beings is demonstrated by the total giving of Himself, holding nothing back! And let us ever keep in mind that we cannot really separate the love of God from the love of The three Persons of our Triune God, namely The Father, The Son, and The Holy Spirit. In other words, it is the love of One God which is in view, being expressed by each Person of our One-in-Three Persons God.

May the truth just shared about the love of our Triune (Three in One) God for the human race penetrate our deepest consciousness, for when it does, it provides the basis for how God wants us to love others with that same love, which one receives from God at the moment of personally coming to know God at salvation, noting what God tells us at Romans 5:5, "and hope does not disappoint, because the love of God has been poured out within our hearts through the Holy Spirit who was given to us." With God's life imparted to us at salvation comes His love also, which we have and demonstrate to others as we walk with God with no known unconfessed sins in our lives. Only sin can interrupt that flow of God's life and of therefore of His love.

That is why God can then say to believers in the second part of 1 John 3:16, as those who have received His love, "We know love by this, that He laid down His life for us; and we ought to lay down our lives for the brethren." Laying down our lives for others here means to love with a total giving of ourselves, with nothing held back. It is the love, for instance, that then provides a basis for a marriage between a man and a woman, and is also the glue that holds a family together! In turn, it is also the glue that holds a society together and allows it to function in harmony.

One last truth to remember here is that God never forces people to love Him, although He does want us to willingly love Him, which we will do once we come to know Him. The more we know God, the more we will love Him. So God's first intent was to demonstrate what His love was like, so that in seeing His love displayed, we would have some idea of what the love He wants us to pass on to others looks like. And that demonstration of God's love was centrally set forth in His own precious Son. After all, The Father's love and The Holy Spirit's love for human beings is invisible to us. We can only read about it in God's words. In other words, God The Father set out to make His Son the VISIBLE model or the example by which His love would be displayed and made known to human beings. God's desire was that in looking at His Son, Who came to this earth as Jesus Christ, and seeing how He lived and then how He died in our place, we would see the full extent of His love for human beings!

Only the person who had been forgiven one's sins by God can fully appreciate the full blessing of what God's forgiveness truly means!

CHAPTER THREE

/ God's love for human beings made the forgiveness of sins available to all

Guilt is a terrible thing. It eats at us and never gives us rest, which we so long for. And guilt is always the result of our sin against God. When God created us, He so constituted us that we would feel guilty whenever we sin. That is one reason why He gave us emotions and a conscience, so that our conscience may rest in peace when we do right and be in the turmoil of guilt when we sin. Let us notice what God says in His word at Romans 2:14,15 regarding His law written on our hearts, which instinctively tells us through our conscience when we have done right and when we have done wrong, "[14] For when Gentiles (that is, non-Jews) who do not have the Law (meaning externally in written form, as do the Jewish people) do instinctively the things of the Law, these, not having the Law, are a law to themselves, [15] in that they show the work of the Law written in their hearts, their conscience bearing witness and their thoughts alternately accusing or else defending them..."

We have seen in the previous chapter that God's love, demonstrated in the total giving of Himself, with noting held back, first provided a basis for Him to forgive the sins of any sinner who comes to Him and believes His good news regarding His precious Son, Jesus Christ. So there is the forgiveness of sins which comes when we first do believe and thereby enter into a personal relationship with God. This is the forgiveness that God has in view when He calls believers to give thanks to Him such as at Colossians 1:12-14, "[12] giving thanks to the Father, who has qualified us to share in the inheritance of the saints in Light. [13] For He rescued us from the domain of darkness, and transferred us to the kingdom of His beloved Son, [14] in whom we have redemption, the forgiveness of sins." At the moment we believe the gospel regarding God's Son, He unites us to Himself in His Son by The Holy Spirit, and forgives us all our sins ever committed against Him since the age of accountability onwards.

But as we have also mentioned already, even when we become children of God at salvation, we can still sin due to still having a sinful nature, which only wants to sin, and which is not removed from us until the time of our redemption, which is when God brings us to Heaven at the second coming of His precious Son, Jesus Christ. And so, until that time arrives, we still do have the forgiveness of sins available to us, same as when we first came to personally know God at salvation. In other words, the death of God's Son is just as adequate to forgive us our sins AFTER the moment of salvation as it was when we were first forgiven all of our sins by God AT the moment of salvation.

That is why God says to believers, who are now His children, what we read in His word at 1 John 1:9 to 2:2, "[1:9] If we confess our sins, He is faithful and righteous to forgive us our sins and to cleanse us from all unrighteousness. [1:10] If we say that we have not sinned, we make Him a liar and His word is not in us. [2:1] My little children, I am writing these things to you so that you may not sin. And if anyone sins, we have an Advocate (One Who speaks on our behalf) with the Father, Jesus Christ the righteous; [2:2] and He Himself (the Son) is the propitiation (that is, the acceptable sacrifice offered to God The Father) for our sins; and not for ours only, but also for those of the whole world." As we see here, the moment we sin as now a believer, confession of that sin to God brings immediate forgiveness based on God's precious Son, Jesus Christ, having already died as payment of the penalty of death due that sin, and this is true for every sin we commit, no matter how terrible it might be. And so, here's what we can expect to find in this regard, further noting what God tells us in His word at Psalm 86:5, "For You, Lord, are good, and ready to forgive, and abundant in lovingkindness to all who call upon You."

But what we are to further see is that confession not only brings forgiveness of sins, but also leads God to remove the guilt of that sin at the moment of forgiving it. Let us notice what God included in His word at Psalm 32:1-5 regarding the confession of king David of old, as to what he discovered as a believer in this matter of the forgiveness of his sins and the removal of the guilt of them, "[1] How blessed (or how happy) is he whose transgression is forgiven, whose sin is covered! [2] How blessed (or how happy) is the man to whom the Lord does not impute iniquity, and in whose spirit there is no deceit! [3] When I kept silent about my sin, my body wasted away through my groaning all day long. [4] For day and night Your hand was heavy upon me; my vitality was drained away as with the fever heat of summer. [5] I acknowledged my sin to You, and my iniquity I did not hide; I said, "I will confess my transgressions to the Lord"; and You forgave the guilt of my sin." Confession of sins keeps us honest before God, Who sees all and knows that we have not only sinned, but exactly what the nature of that sin was. In other words, we need to confess because God already knows the whole truth, which we cannot hide from Him. If we want to walk with Him, Who is Holy, that is, without sin, then we must walk blamelessly, with no known unconfessed sins in our lives after salvation.

But you may have read this far in this chapter and wonder to yourself, how does this relate to the love of God for human beings? The answer to be grasped here is that the love of God for human beings, as the total giving of Himself we have noted in the second chapter, which led God to give His only begotten Son and which in turn led God's precious Son, Jesus Christ, to give Himself freely as a ransom for sinners at the cross, is where the forgiveness of sins flows from! In other words, there would never be any forgiveness of sins for human beings in time unless God had taken that first step of showing human beings the full extent of His love in totally giving Himself for us in the death of His precious Son, Jesus Christ, at the cross! Let us notice what God tells us in His word at Romans 5:8 in this regard, "But God demonstrates His own love toward us, in that while we were yet sinners, Christ died for us." And so that is what the title to this chapter means when we say, 'God's love for human beings made the forgiveness of sins available to all.'

Even beyond this, we are also to notice that it takes love to forgive another of wrongs done against us. So every time we sin and God forgives us, it is a fresh demonstration of His love for us! And this is the love which God appeals to when He calls believers to forgive others just as He Himself has forgiven us, noting what God tells us in His word at Ephesians 4:32, "Be kind to one another, tender-hearted, forgiving each other, just as God in Christ also has forgiven you." The forgiveness of our sins by God not only enables us, as those who are believers, to walk with Him, Who is without sin, but as we will now see in the next chapter, it also enables us to live the same supernatural life which God ever lives.

At our birth into this world, God gave us physical life that we may live on earth. At salvation, God gave us His own eternal life that we may live with Him now on earth, and later forever in Heaven!

CHAPTER FOUR

/ God's love for human beings made eternal life available to all

In the first chapter, we looked at what God wanted to accomplish when He first created human beings and placed them on this earth, which was to display the full extent of His love to those human beings. And it is obvious that in order for God to accomplish this, then He had to first, in love, provide for the forgiveness of sins, and then secondly, He had to continually impart His life, the same eternal life He ever lives, to those forgiven human beings, so that they might be enabled to walk with Him blamelessly, that is, without known unconfessed sins. Therefore, the second benefit which God's love as a total giving of Himself provides for human beings is eternal life. Since God is an eternal Being, Who has ever existed and will forever exist, then the life He provides to any sinner who believes the good news regarding His Son, is eternal life. And how important that we see that this life only flows from God due to the love of God shown as a total giving of Himself, which was demonstrated at its fullest when God's precious Son, Jesus Christ, died at the cross for the sins of all human beings of time.

And what is important to ever remember about this eternal life, which is God's own life, or righteousness, is that it is first imputed to us (that is, reckoned to us as ours) at the moment of salvation, when The precious Holy Spirit first comes to indwell our human spirit at the moment of our believing the message of the gospel relating to God's precious Son. After that initial moment, God continually imparts His life (that is, shares with those who are now His children) as one walks with Him blamelessly, that is, with no unconfessed sins in one's life. Every believer carries one's own confessional at all times, which is 1 John 1:9, "If we confess our sins, He is faithful and righteous to forgive us our sins and to cleanse us from all unrighteousness." So whenever we sin, we sense it right away due to The Holy Spirit in our spirit letting our conscience know that we have sinned, also giving us that guilt feeling, so that we lose our peace and joy with God until such time as we confess our sin to God.

What is important to ever keep in mind here is that we never lose that eternal life from God, even when we sin, because God now eternally indwells us in our human spirit through His Son by His Holy Spirit. At the moment we believed the message God gave regarding His Son and received The Holy Spirit, we became children of God, which is forever. Same as children born to a set of parents in this world cannot ever stop being their child, no matter how many wrongs against one's parents one may do; the same is true in regards to those who become God's children at salvation. They can never stop being a child of God, no matter how terrible the sin may be that one sins against God. Forgiveness, which God Himself provides based on the death of His own precious Son, Jesus Christ, on behalf of sinners, is always available the moment the child of God confesses one's sin to God. And likewise the flow of the eternal life which God provides at salvation, due to the death of God's precious Son on behalf of sinners, is only interrupted at the moment of one's sin and is resumed again the moment one confesses one's sin to God.

So let us praise God for the love that He has shown to the human race in making eternal life with Himself available to all human beings through the death at the cross of His precious Son on our behalf, as our Substitute, to pay the penalty of death due the sins of all human beings. As we close, let us be aware that this is the love that God uses to then spur us as believers to live by the life that He Himself ever lives, noting what God tells us at 1 Peter 2:24, "and He Himself bore our sins in His body on the cross, that we might die to sin and live to righteousness; for by His wounds you were healed." When God says here, "die to sin" He is making reference to our sinful nature, so that God is in effect saying to us, 'My Son bore your sins at the cross, so that now you would willingly turn away from your sinful nature, as the source of your sins, and live only to display the life of God, His righteousness, which He wants you to live by instead.'

It is a mind-boggling truth, but nonetheless true, that we would never know the love of God apart from believing in His Son for salvation, through Whom God's love ever comes!

CHAPTER FIVE

/ God's love is to be seen as always being in and through His Son

God's love for the human race was not only made possible through the death of God's own precious Son on behalf of all human beings under the condemnation of death due to sin, but God's love is always only found in, and given to us by God through, God's precious Son by The Holy Spirit! The reason for this is due to God The Father, Who is a spirit Being (John 4:24), always indwelling His Son by The Holy Spirit and also always working through His Son by The Holy Spirit, whether acting or speaking. And here we can note what The Son was led of His Father to say at John 14:10,24, "[10] Do you not believe that I am in the Father, and the Father is in Me? The words that I say to you I do not speak on My own initiative, but the Father abiding in Me does His works... [14] He who does not love Me does not keep My words; and the word which you hear is not Mine, but the Father's who sent Me."

We must again remember that there is only One God, although revealed to us in three Persons, as Father, Son, and Holy Spirit. And also that The Son is ever the VISIBLE expression of God, Who is invisible (John 1:18; 1 Timothy 6:16). As God The Father says at Colossians 1:15, "He (The Son) is the image of the invisible God." So God's love, as is also true of God's life, can only come to human beings from God The Father through His Son by The Holy Spirit. Let us notice what God tells us in His word at Romans 8:38,39, "[38] For I am convinced that neither death, nor life, nor angels, nor principalities, nor things present, nor things to come, nor powers, [39] nor height, nor depth, nor any other created thing, will be able to separate us from the love of God, which is IN Christ Jesus our Lord."

God makes another very revealing statement in His word at Romans 8:32, when He says "He (God The Father) who did not spare His own Son, but delivered Him over for us all, how will He not also with Him freely give us all things?" The "all things" which God freely gives us has His life and His love at the top of the list, which we now know is due to the death of God's own Son on our behalf, and is also through God's own Son, by The Holy Spirit. And the "us," repeated here twice, refers only to those who are now children of God in salvation, as those who have believed the message of the gospel which God gave regarding His Son, namely that He died for our sins, was buried, and then was raised the third day from the dead. In looking at God's Son in the word of God, we not only see the fullness of God on display (Colossians 2:9), but we also see the full display of the love of God for human beings!

The test of whether we love God or not is whether we love other human beings or not!

CHAPTER SIX

/ God's love is to be the basis for our loving other human beings

It should not surprise us that God intends His love, which was given fullest expression in and through His Son, to be the basis for our loving other human beings! Let us note what God says in His word at 1 John 4:19,20, "[19] We love, because He first loved us. [20] If someone says, "I love God," and hates his brother, he is a liar; for the one who does not love his brother whom he has seen, cannot love God whom he has not seen." Here we see that our love to others should flow from the love that God has first of all shown us, and also that our love for God will be shown by whether we love other human beings or not. In other words, God wants to see some practicality to our love; some visible demonstration of our love to others, which proves that we indeed love God with the love by which He loves us!

We cannot just say that we love God or that we love other human beings, we have to demonstrate it, as God demonstrated His own love for human beings in a practical way, which was in giving us His own Son to die in our place. And so that is why God says to His own at 1 John 3:17,18, "[17] But whoever has the world's goods, and sees his brother in need and closes his heart against him, how does the love of God abide in him? [18] Little children, let us not love with word or with tongue, but in deed and truth." Just as God's love for us was anchored in the realism of life, in that either God intervened to provide for our redemption, or else the whole human race would have been separated from Him eternally; so too with us, God wants our love for others to be anchored in the realism of life, to be practical

39

in terms of meeting needs where people live their daily lives. As God says here, love is to be more than just words!

Before leaving this chapter, let us also note that when God says at 1 John 4:19 above, "We love, because He first loved us," that God's love in view here always has the love that He showed us in and through His own Son, when He gave Him to die instead of us. In other words, the words "He first loved us" refers back to the death of God's precious Son at the cross. This is especially clear if we note what God also says to us in His word at 1 John 4:10,11, "[10] In this is love, not that we loved God, but that He loved us and sent His Son to be the propitiation (that is, the acceptable sacrifice offered to God) for our sins. [11] Beloved, if God so loved us, we also ought to love one another." What we have just said above is clear from verse 11 here, in that the death of God's Son on behalf of sinners of time is central to God's love. In other words, God's love for human beings is always anchored in the love demonstrated by His Son when He died in our place. And then as we see at verse 11, that love by which God loved us, which was a total giving of Himself, holding nothing back, is the love that God wants us to also demonstrate to others in more than just words!

Love begets love; and love demonstrated in action begets love demonstrated in action!

CHAPTER SEVEN

/ God's love is to be the basis for keeping a marriage relationship going

God's love, as demonstrated in the death of His precious Son on our behalf, is also used by God as a basis for keeping a marriage relationship going, seeing at Ephesians 5:25 how God appeals to the husband, as the one having the primary responsibility for demonstrating God's love to his wife, "Husbands, love your wives, just as Christ also loved the church and gave Himself up for her..." The death of God's precious Son, Jesus Christ, at the cross, is here in view in the words, "Christ also loved... and gave Himself up..." God then uses the love demonstrated by His Son to appeal to believing husbands to then show that same love to their wives, meaning that love that gives all of oneself for another, holding nothing back; which one has from the moment of salvation onwards (Romans 5:5), and which God continually goes on to impart with His life as we live with no known unconfessed sins in our lives.

When a husband does this, in terms of displaying this type of all-giving love to his wife, then he will find that the truth of 1 John 4:19 will also be true in his marriage relationship, "We love, because He first loved us." Now it will be, 'the wife loves, because he, her husband, first loved her.' Love begets love, and the demonstration of God's love to another brings forth the same demonstration of God's love. So we can say then, as was briefly mentioned earlier in the book, that God's love is the glue that keeps a marriage, and subsequently a family, together.

When God says to parents at Proverbs 22:6, "Train up a child in the way he should go, even when he is old he will not depart from it,"

God has more than rules and regulations in mind. God has a way of life in mind, which is undergirded by the love of God. In other words, a child brought up in a home where God's love was demonstrated by one's parents, will cause the child to want and go out to establish the same kind of home. This is what God had in mind for Adam and Eve originally, and therefore for the whole human race, namely to have a man and woman on earth who believed in Him, and after learning what God's love is like, through a demonstration of it and then through personal appropriation, would then pass on that love to their children, who in turn would set up similar believing homes, established on the love of God. Unfortunately, that did not happen as originally intended by God due to sin, which is also the case in most marriages today, in that sin will also often prevent God's love from being demonstrated and passed on from generation to generation.

A bondslave is a slave that is in willing service to one's master due to loving that master. This is what God wants us to willingly become after salvation. And this is what we will indeed become once the love of God grips us!

CHAPTER EIGHT

/ God's love is to be the basis for our service to God

What we have seen so far is just how far-reaching the love of God really is, as demonstrated when His precious Son gave Himself unto death for us at the cross. But God is not done teaching us. In this chapter, we will discover that His love is also to be the basis for our service to Him, noting what God tells us at 2 Corinthians 5:14,15, "[14] For the love of Christ controls us, having concluded this, that one died for all, therefore all died; [15] and He died for all, so that they who live might no longer live for themselves, but for Him who died and rose again on their behalf." By now, we should all know what God means when He speaks of "the love of Christ" in the first part of verse 14, when He says that "One died for all" and "He died for all." In other words, God again makes reference to the full extent of the love of God for human beings in the death of His precious Son, when He gave Himself over to death at the cross, bearing there our sins in His own body, that God would have a basis for forgiving the sins of anyone who subsequently believes in Him.

And as we see in the last part of verse 15, God then uses the love of Christ, as shown in His death for us at the cross, as the basis for serving Him, when He says, "and He died for all, so that they who live might no longer live for themselves, but for Him who died and rose again on their behalf." The "they who live" here are believers, as those who have experienced the love of God at salvation. These are to no longer live for one's self in living by one's sinful nature, but rather, "for Him who died and rose again on their behalf." This will not have a full impact upon our lives here until we realize what God's Son did His whole life long at His first coming from Heaven to earth, which was as He gives testimony to at John 6:38, "For I have come down from heaven, not to do My own will, but the will of Him who sent Me." To serve another is to do the will of another. And so, in God's Son doing only His Father's will meant that He always served Him, and that as a Pattern for us.

What this means then in terms of what God says to us as believers at 2 Corinthians 5:15 above is that since we have now personally experienced through salvation the love of God as demonstrated in His precious Son at the cross, we are no longer to serve ourselves, by seeking to carry out our own will in daily living, but rather we are to show our love to God by carrying out His will instead. If we were to read the rest of the chapter, namely all of 2 Corinthians 5, we would discover that God wants us who are believers to be vessels in His Hands, to reach other people with the gospel. As one writer once stated it, 'we have been saved in order to serve God.'

And so that is what God intends when He says at the beginning of 2 Corinthians 5:14 above, 'For the love of Christ controls us..." In other words, God wants His love, as demonstrated in the death of His Son on our behalf, to be what grips us, so that it then causes us to willingly want to serve Him out of love for Him. That is the purest kind of service, that serves based on the love of God, not service that is given as one's perceived duty, or service where one thinks of obtaining God's favor by it, but rather, service that has no other goal but to love as He loves, as demonstrated for us by His Son, Jesus Christ. This is what God regards as a bondslave, meaning one who is not forced to serve Him, but who does so willingly out of love for Him, once one has personally experienced the love of God as demonstrated by His Son when He died for us at the cross. And this type of bondslave is what God wants all believers to become after having experienced salvation, noting what He tells us at Colossians 4:12, "Epaphras, who is one of your number, a bondslave of Jesus Christ, sends you his greetings, always laboring earnestly for you in his prayers, that you may stand perfect and fully assured in all the will of God."

"Through Him (God's Son, Jesus Christ) then, let us continually offer up a sacrifice of praise to God, that is, the fruit of lips that give thanks to His name."

Hebrews 13:15

CHAPTER NINE

/ God's love is the basis for our worship of God

God's love, which was given its fullest expression and demonstration in the death of His precious Son at the cross, when He died in our place, paying the penalty of death due our sin, is to also be seen as being the basis for our worship of God. And what is important to keep in mind at the outset is that worship is simply giving God His worth, which is best done through the adoration of praise and thanksgiving, when we consider all that God has done for us, which is again to be seen as centered in the death of His own precious Son, Jesus Christ, on our behalf. And the observance that God specifically instituted to do this, namely giving Him the worship He deserves while considering the fullest extent of His love for us, is The Lord's Supper, or what some refer to as 'Communion,' or 'a Love Feast,' or 'the Remembrance Supper.'

Let us note what God led the apostle Paul to write at 1 Corinthians 11:23-26 regarding The Lord's Supper, "[23] For I received from the Lord that which I also delivered to you, that the Lord Jesus in the night in which He was betrayed took bread; [24] and when He had given thanks, He broke it, and said, "This is My body, which is for you; do this in remembrance of Me." [25] In the same way He took the cup also, after supper, saying, "This cup is the new covenant in My blood; do this, as often as you drink it, in remembrance of Me." [26] For as often as you eat this bread and drink the cup, you proclaim the Lord's death until He comes." As we see here, The Lord's Supper, which God instituted for believers, is to be a time of remembrance, focused on one central theme, which was the love of God as demonstrated in the death of His precious Son on our behalf.

As we partake of the bread and the cup together, which speaks of the body of the Son of God willingly given over unto death on a cross on our behalf, out of love for us, we are to remember that His death was for us, as undeserving sinners, which God then applied to our lives personally at salvation. And in remembering the love of God centered in the cross, specifically what it cost God in the giving of His own Son, God Himself leads us in worship through the adoration of praise and thanksgiving by His Holy Spirit in us. This can be achieved silently in prayer or through corporate prayer; or through the singing of hymns, which are often termed 'hymns of worship,' simply because they contain in them the expression of praise and thanksgiving that wells up in our hearts as we remember the full extent of God's love for us in His precious Son, Jesus Christ!

God is a gift-giver at heart, which is why He tells us that "it is more blessed to give than to receive" (Acts 20:35).

CHAPTER TEN

/ God's love is to be seen as a gift we do not deserve

Even though God does not directly say in His word that His love is a gift, we nevertheless indirectly know that it is due to what God says about salvation, which is a gift, noting what God says in His word at Ephesians 2;8,9, [8] For by grace you have been saved through faith; and that not of yourselves, it is the gift of God; [9] not as a result of works, so that no one may boast." So anyone reading this who is saved, in terms of having believed the gospel God gave regarding His precious Son, is so because of having received the gift of God, which is the faith to believe, resulting in salvation, which is the moment one enters into a personal relationship with God.

The reason salvation is a gift is that it comes directly from God by grace, which is His unmerited favor towards us. In other words, we do not deserve it, nor have we earned it. As God points out at verse 9 above, salvation is not by works, that is, not based on anything we have done; but rather it is based solely on what God has done for us, when in love for us He gave His precious and only Son unto death for us, and when His precious Son died willingly in our place. And so, God's love is a gift in the sense that it comes to us as part of God's salvation to us, which is a gift. Salvation can therefore be viewed as the gift, while God's love can be looked at as the wrapping salvation comes to us in!

But that is not all God has to say about His love being a gift. We can also note what He tells us in His word at Ephesians 1:4,5, "[4] just as He (God The Father) chose us (those who become believers in time) in Him (His Son) before the foundation of the world (before creation even took place and time began), that we would be holy and blameless before Him (one day at a future time). In love [5] He predestined us to adoption as sons through Jesus Christ to Himself, according to the kind intention of His will..." There is a lot of important truth here! The first is that God chose those who are saved in time before the foundation of the world, before we were even created in Adam, the first man. That this is so can also be grasped from what God tells us in His word at 2 Thessalonians 2:13,14, [13] But we should always give thanks to God for you, brethren beloved by the Lord, because God has chosen you from the beginning for salvation through sanctification (that is, being set apart for God's use) by the Spirit and faith in the truth. [14] It was for this He called you through our gospel, that you may gain the glory of our Lord Jesus Christ."

The second truth that we see at the end of Ephesians 1:4 above is that it was out of love for us that God did this, in terms of choosing those who are saved in time from before the foundation of the world. When we read at the end of verse 15 that He did this "out of the kind intention of His will," we are to realize that this means we were not involved at all in that decision, that this was wholly something that God decided on His own! And so, when we read at Ephesians 1:4,5, "In love He predestined us to adoption as sons through Jesus Christ," we are to understand that what God basically means here is that those chosen of God to be His in time from before the foundation of the world are destined to be children in God's family when that moment of salvation does come at some point in time.

As a further help to those who may not be familiar with this term "adoption as sons," we need to know that this takes place in two stages in time. In other words, becoming a child of God, which is what "adoption as sons" refers to, is to be seen as taking place in two stages. The first stage of our adoption into God's family is at the moment of our salvation, which takes place at some moment in time, noting what God says about this first stage at Romans 8:15,16, "[15] For you have not received a spirit (should be 'Spirit') of slavery leading to fear again, but you have received a spirit (should be 'Spirit') of adoption as sons by which we cry out, "Abba! Father!" [16] The Spirit Himself testifies with our spirit that we are children of God..." And so we see here that at the moment of our salvation, the Holy Spirit, Who comes to indwell our human spirit, makes us realize internally in a spiritual way that we have just become children of God.

He makes us realize the reality of it, so that it is unmistakable and cannot be missed.

Then the second stage of our adoption as sons is spoken of by God at Romans 8:23, "And not only this, but also we ourselves, having the first fruits of the Spirit, even we ourselves groan within ourselves, waiting eagerly for our adoption as sons, the redemption of our body." It is clear then, from what God says here, that our adoption as sons, that is, that the process of our fully becoming children of God through salvation, is not completed until the time of the redemption of our body. What God has in view here is the fact that we cannot enter Heaven with the present bodies that we have. God needs to change that body so that it will last forever, in terms of never being subject to decay and death anymore. What this means then is that the "redemption of our body" here refers to the time of the first resurrection relating to believers, when one is raised from the dead by God and given a new body to last forever with Him in Heaven.

In order to not lose anyone in the details here, please note two passages in particular where God speaks about this, the first being at 1 Corinthians 15:42-44, "[42] So also is the resurrection of the dead. It is sown a perishable body, it is raised an imperishable body; [43] it is sown in dishonor, it is raised in glory; it is sown in weakness, it is raised in power; [44] it is sown a natural body, it is raised a spiritual body. If there is a natural body, there is also a spiritual body." And the second passage being what God says at Philippians 3:20,21, "[20] For our citizenship is in heaven, from which also we eagerly wait for a Savior, the Lord Jesus Christ; [21] who will transform the body of our humble state into conformity with the body of His glory, by the exertion of the power that He has even to subject all things to Himself."

We may have gone slightly afield from our topic here for a moment in discussing the term "adoption as sons," which I am sure all will agree was worthwhile, but the truth that must be grasped from all this is that it was out of love that God predestined us to be adopted as His children from before the foundation of the world! And it was not something that we deserved, for as we have seen already, the whole human race went into sin from Adam onwards, so that if we had been left to ourselves, we would never see Heaven. Note for instance what God's assessment of the human race is from what we read at

Romans 3:10-12,23 in parts, "[10] There is none righteous, not even one... [11] There is none who seeks for God... [12] There is none who does good, not even one... [23] For all have sinned and fall short of the glory of God..." The sad reality is that God had to intervene, out of His love for human beings, and it was also out of love for that human race that God did send His Son in time to die for al human beings, that those He chose in love before time began could be saved in time through his death, burial, and resurrection from the dead! This is again a truth worth remembering and giving God praise and thanks for! Amen?

The purest form of love is unconditional, which only God can give.

CHAPTER ELEVEN

/ God's love is to be seen as being unconditional

When God loves, he does not attach any conditions to His love. And this is what many find hard to believe, especially when one has sinned and is full of guilt. The thought that many then have is: How can God forgive me for that? But we always need to remember that God is God and we are not, so that He does not think or do as we do, noting what God says at Isaiah 55:8,9 in this regard, "[8] For My thoughts are not your thoughts, nor are your ways My ways," declares the Lord. [9] For as the heavens are higher than the earth, so are My ways higher than your ways and My thoughts than your thoughts.""

And the reason for our thinking as we do is that we are so used to the concept of retribution, which says that the guilty should pay for the consequence of the wrong done. And so, when we sin that means we are guilty before God and therefore we deserve God's punishment due our sin. However, as we have seen already, this is where God's love came in. The guilty can go free from the penalty of death due one's sins by believing in The Substitute, which is God's own precious Son, Jesus Christ, Whom The Father gave to die in our place the death that was due our sins. And when we do believe, by God's grace and power, and therefore are forgiven all our sins, even being made the very children of God, then it is just as we have seen at Romans 8:1 already, there is no condemnation for those who are in Christ Jesus. That is, God's wrath against us is turned to love the moment we became His child at salvation. And since this is a work which God has done, then we can be sure that God's love for us is unconditional. That is, nothing that we can think, say, or do will make God stop loving us, once we are His children.

But one may ask: How do we really know that God loves us, His children, unconditionally? Does God tell us this in His word? Actually, God does not tell us this in a direct statement, but He does give us clues that He loves us unconditionally from some of the truths that He shares with us. For instance, God's precious Son, Jesus Christ, said what we read at John 15:9 to His followers one day, who were believers, "Just as the Father has loved Me, I have also loved you; abide in My love." And before commenting in this statement, let us notice another truth which God's precious Son has shared, this time at John 17:23, where we have The Son speaking to His Father in prayer, "I in them and You in Me, that they may be perfected in unity, so that the world may know that You sent Me, and loved them, even as You have loved Me."

And so we see first at John 15:9 the stupendous truth that God's Son loves believers "just as The Father has loved Me." Now, can one doubt that God The Father loves His Son unconditionally? Of course, not. There is no doubt in my mind and heart at least that God The Father has always loved His precious Son unconditionally, and ever will. And this is the same love we are loved with by The Son, which has to be unconditionally also. Then at John 17:23, the truth being shared there is that believers are loved by God The Father with the same love with which He loves His own precious Son, Jesus Christ. As we have just seen, since the love of God is unconditional, then the love He extends to His human creation after salvation is also unconditional. Amazing unconditional love it is!

And because God loves us unconditionally, he wants us to love others in the same way, since we are now His children and represent Him in the world. This means that He expects His own to show the family likeness. That is why God says at Luke 6:32 for instance, "If you love those who love you, what credit is that to you? For even sinners (meaning unbelievers) love those who love them." That is also why God's precious Son, Jesus Christ, told His followers while He was on earth what we read at John 13:34,35, "[34] A new commandment I give to you, that you love one another, even as I have loved you, that you also love one another. [35] By this all men will know that you are My disciples, if you have love for one another."

But the love that God's Son was asking believers to love by was not the same love as those who were unbelievers were loving others by, which was to love only those who loved them. Rather, God's precious Son wanted those who were part of the family of God to love as they themselves had been loved by God at salvation, which is unconditionally, which of course is not something that is natural to us. Let us notice at Ephesians 5:1,2 what God calls us to who are His own, "[1] Therefore be imitators of God, as beloved children; [2] and walk in love, just as Christ also loved you and gave Himself up for us, an offering and a sacrifice to God as a fragrant aroma." That is why God imparts us His life to live by at the time of salvation onwards, for when we live by His life, which we will do when we live with no known unconfessed sins in our lives, then we are enabled by God's grace and power, through His Holy Spirit in us, to love unconditionally, even loving those who to us are naturally unlovable.

Knowing that we are loved brings peace and security to our souls.

CHAPTER TWELVE

/ God's love is the basis for our sense of security and peace while on earth

All of us have no doubt observed, at one time or another, an infant just barely walking, who when in public, all of a sudden sees someone who is unknown or whom they are uncertain of. The child's first reaction is to scurry to mom, wherever she may be. Why? Because that is where the infant's sense of security and peace based on love is. She is the one the infant has an imprint of. What is meant here is that for nine months two hearts were linked together, so that the infant grew to know that one other heartbeat apart from its own. For nine months mom was the infant's provider and sense of security. Whatever love the child knows, it was picked up from the mother. And because the infant knows nothing but the mother's unconditional love, there being no uncertainty about it since rejection is as yet an unknown factor, then the child does what comes naturally in scurrying back to mom, at the least hint of a threat of any kind.

Now let us apply this same truth to God our Father. The moment we come to know Him at salvation, we are united to Him through His Son by The Holy Spirit, and imparted His life (Romans 8:11), along with His love (Romans 5:5). From that moment onwards, God assures us that we have peace with Him, noting what He tells us at Romans 5:1, "Therefore having been justified by faith, we have peace with God through our Lord Jesus Christ..." Having been made right with God at the moment we believed in God's Son, which is when God forgave us all our sins and gave us His own life (righteousness) to live by, we experienced the peace that only God can give, which passes all understanding. We also instinctively knew that unmistakable peace and sense of security, due to God's felt Presence and the knowledge that He loved us and accepted us as we were. Let us notice what we read at 1 John 4:16a for instance, "We have come to know and believed the love which God has for us."

As we grow in the grace and knowledge of God by reading His word on a daily basis, we discover further assurances from God that we are safe with Him when we read eternal truth such as at Deuteronomy 33:27a, "The eternal God is a dwelling place (refuge), and underneath are the everlasting arms...," and also at Romans 8:1, "Therefore there is now no condemnation for those who are in Christ Jesus." Since we have believed in God's precious Son, Jesus Christ, for salvation, as The One Who in love gave Himself to die in our place, namely that He paid the penalty for our sins, then we can rest assured in the peace and security that we will never have to face God in judgment due to our sins against Him in time.

No matter what befalls us in this life, we know, due to knowing that God loves us unconditionally, that we can come to Him at any time and there find a refuge from the raging of the storm of life that we may be going through. In other words, it is knowing that God loves us and being secure in that love, which leads us to seek Him as our refuge in a time of need. What needs to be remembered here is that it is because of God's love for us that this is so, in terms of His ever being a ready refuge for us, noting again what God says at Romans 8:32, "He who did not spare His own Son, but delivered Him over for us all, how will He not also with Him freely give us all things?"

Since God loves us this much, then we can be sure that God will be there as our safe haven in a time of uncertainty and need. And here we can note two of God's promises in this regard, the one being at Psalm 27:5, "For in the day of trouble He will conceal me in His tabernacle; in the secret place of His tent He will hide me; He will lift me up on a rock," and also at Psalm 40:1,2, "[1] I waited patiently for the Lord; and He inclined to me and heard my cry. [2] He brought me up out of the pit of destruction, out of the miry clay, and He set my feet upon a rock making my footsteps firm." It is for good reason that God is called "The God of love and peace" at 2 Corinthians 13:11, and also why He says to us, as His children, what we read at 2

Thessalonians 2:16,17, "[16] Now may our Lord Jesus Christ Himself and God our Father, who has loved us and given us eternal comfort and good hope by grace, [17] comfort and strengthen your hearts in every good work and word."

Humbleness will lead us to prayer, but pride will keep us from it!

CHAPTER THIRTEEN

/ God's love means we have a shoulder to cry on and a place to lay our burdens

I do not mind disclosing that where I cry the most is on God's shoulder, for after well over thirty-five years of knowing Him in salvation, I have no doubt that He loves me unconditionally and that I can come to Him at any time of day or night and there find a ready listening ear to unburden myself to. After all, prayer is nothing more than a child of God coming to The precious Father and conversing with Him regarding all that is going on in one's life. It is the same as what we used to do as children, when we lived at home, running to our parents and finding there a loving heart that was always ready to not only hear, but also to comfort and counsel, in accordance with the need of the moment. Unlike our parents, who were far less than perfect, and were not always available, God is perfect so that He cannot be improved upon, while at the same time never gone somewhere where He is not accessible, nor does He ever sleep.

God even tells us that this is what He wants us to do when we are burdened and need a shoulder to cry on, noting what we read at Philippians 4:6, 'Be anxious for nothing, but in everything by prayer and supplication with thanksgiving let your requests be made known to God," and also at 1 Peter 5:7, "casting all your anxiety on Him, because He cares for you." He Who loved us so much that He did not even spare His own Son, but gave Him up for us, how will He not along with Him give us all things (Romans 8:32), which no doubt includes a shoulder to cry on and an ear to listen, day or night. It is humbling to pray, but when we know The One Who loves us awaits us, there is no pride to prevent us from coming to God.

It is only when we ourselves have had our burdens lifted by God, out of love for us, first at the moment of salvation, and thereafter every time we have needed it, that we can then be vessels in God's Hands to help brothers and sisters in the family of God, noting what God tells us at 2 Corinthians 1:3,4, "[3] Blessed be the God and Father of our Lord Jesus Christ, the Father of mercies and God of all comfort, [4] who comforts us in all our affliction so that we will be able to comfort those who are in any affliction with the comfort with which we ourselves are comforted by God." After all, it is difficult to pass on to others what we have never experienced ourselves.

We cannot hoard God's love. Once we become a recipient of it, we will want to pass it on to others!

CHAPTER FOURTEEN

/ God's love is given to be shared with others

When God first saved His servant on January 14, 1980, I then became involved with a businessmen's group whose sole purpose for existing was to share one's faith with other businessmen. One person who often met with us was the captain of the Salvation Army in that city. This man, who at the time was about sixty years of age, so exuded the love of God that every person who met him was instantly attracted to him. It was therefore not surprising to hear much later, from another man who had been saved under this man's ministry, that many people were brought to faith in God through him. He led his congregation in the operation of a coffee house for teens in our city, where musicians from the Salvation Army and others regularly played. Since I was not a teen, this was something that I had only heard about, but had not paid much attention to. But as it turned out, this captain used to circulate among the teens at the coffee house and as a result many of them became believers. When I heard this, the one thought which struck me then, even though I was still a relatively new believer, was that the love of God this man demonstrated must have been what God used in his life to first attract these teens to him, and then God used the gospel he shared to save them.

The above true story was written here to bring out the truth that once we experience the love of God in salvation and are filled with His love, then we will want to pass it on to others, that they too may benefit by it, whether that be for someone to also come to know God, or whether that be for a believer who at that moment needs the comforting love of God. Let us notice what God says to His own at 2 Corinthians 5:21-6:2, here as relating to being vessels in God's

Hands, so that others might come to know Him through us, "[5:21] He made Him who knew no sin to be sin on our behalf, so that we might become the righteousness of God in Him. [6:1] And working together with Him, we also urge you not to receive the grace of God in vain — [2] for He says, "At the acceptable time I listened to you, and on the day of salvation I helped you." Behold, now is "the acceptable time," behold, now is "the day of salvation." " As we see at verse 21 here, God uses the love of God as shown in the death of His own precious Son on our behalf as the basis to call believers to be vessels of righteousness in the Hands of God, to bring His love as seen in the gospel to those who do not as yet believe.

And what is important to be aware of here is that there are many ways in which God can use us as vessels in His Hands. For instance, we could be a musician, either writing our own songs under God's guiding Hand, or else singing someone else's songs, which point people to the love of God in the death of God's own Son, so as to eventually hear the gospel and come to know God in a personal relationship. One might even have a website, where the way of salvation is made known; or even a Facebook page. Actually, these two ways are very commonly used today. And of course, one can write Christian books, same as the author has done under God's guiding Hand and under His direction. God is not ever limited in ways of sharing His truth when we do not limit Him. Not everyone is called and sent out as an evangelist, but everyone whom God calls to Himself in salvation is expected to share the love of God by sharing one's faith, as God leads.

Let us look at God's promises as being secret love notes which He sends to those who are His children!

CHAPTER FIFTEEN

/ Seeing God's promises as being secret love notes which He sends to His own!

We do not often think as the promises of God found in His word as being secret love notes which He sends to those who are His children on earth. Since God's promises are not meant for anyone but His own - meaning not meant for unbelievers, for instance - then they should be viewed as God's expression of His care and love for us, meant to comfort and encourage us while we sojourn on this earth, which is not our home.

To begin with, let us look at Psalm 103:1-5, where we see God give five great and precious promises as an indication of His love for us, noting what we there read, "'[1] Bless the Lord, O my soul, and all that is within me, bless His holy name. [2] Bless the Lord, O my soul, and forget none of His benefits; [3] Who pardons all your iniquities, Who heals all your diseases; [4] Who redeems your life from the pit, Who crowns you with lovingkindness and compassion; [5] Who satisfies your years with good things, so that your youth is renewed like the eagle."

One thing we can note from what we read here at verses 3 to 5 is that such great and precious promises touches us at the core of our being, so that no believer would want to be without them once they do touch us in this way, no doubt this being a work of God's grace and power in love when that happens! Which child of God would not delight in the knowledge of sins forgiven, of diseases healed, of having been redeemed from the pit of hell, of having experienced the touch of God's love and compassion, and of finding satisfaction in God's will with each passing year, so that one's youth is renewed?

Another thing that we can state here is that not all of God's promises can be fully understood by God's children, since we are all at various stages of spiritual growth. Some were born into God's family only yesterday, while others have been children of God for decades. So while we can probably all identify with the first four promises quite readily, and even with the first part of verse 5, where we read, "Who satisfies your years with good things," however, the second part of the verse many might only gaze at and stand in wonderment, where we read, "so that your youth is renewed like the eagle." For after all, God does speak of the span of "years" here.

As a help, we can look at one other Scripture passage, which can shed light on this, and where we also see God's great and precious promises, that being at Isaiah 40:27-31, where we read, "[27] Why do you say, O Jacob, and assert, O Israel, "My way is hidden from the Lord, and the justice due me escapes the notice of my God"? [28] Do you not know? Have you not heard? The Everlasting God, the Lord, the Creator of the ends of the earth does not become weary or tired. His understanding is inscrutable. [29] He gives strength to the weary, and to him who lacks might He increases power. [30] Though youths grow weary and tired, and vigorous young men stumble badly, [31] Yet those who wait for the Lord will gain new strength; they will mount up with wings like eagles, they will run and not get tired, they will walk and not become weary."

Here we note that at verse 30 we have the mention of youths, then young men, with the inference at verse 31 being that with God there is hope, even for the older folks, of gaining new strength, of mounting up with wings like eagles, of walking and not getting wearied, of running and not getting tired, which complements what we read at the last part of Psalm 103:5 above. One Biblical example we can mention here is Moses, noting what is written of him at Deuteronomy 34:7 when he died at the age of 120, "Although Moses was one hundred and twenty years old when he died, his eye was not dim, nor his vigor abated." Therefore, what we read at Psalm 103:5 and Isaiah 40:31 certainly appears to have applied to Moses during his lifetime, in terms of having his years satisfied with good things, no doubt as part of God's love for one of His own.

One of the truths that this chapter brings out is that God's love for us is practical in nature. We have noted earlier on what God asks of us at 1 John 3:18, which is to love with more than just words. Well, that is what God Himself practices day in and day out. All that we receive from God, from the air we breathe to all our provisions to sustain our life here on earth, are to be seen as a practical expression of God's love for us! One thing we can be sure of in this life is that human beings will disappoint us at one time or another, but we can be equally sure of this, that God's love will never disappoint us!

"See how great a love the Father has bestowed on us, that we would be called children of God..."

1 John 3:1 in part

CHAPTER SIXTEEN

/ When we come in contact with God's love, we come in contact with God Himself!

One truth that we probably do not often ponder, unless God makes us aware of it, such as with this book now, is that when we come in contact with God's love, we are actually in contact with God Himself. Let us note what God says to us at 1 John 4:12 for instance, "No one has seen God at any time; if we love one another, God abides in us, and His love is perfected in us." As was mentioned earlier, God The Father is invisible to us (1 Timothy 6:16), but when we love one another with His love, which He imparts to us at salvation (Romans 5:5), then we are touching God Himself, both the one who is loving with His love and the one being loved with His love. It is then that His love is perfected in us, in the sense that it is in its exercise that we come to see the reality of it and the beauty of its perfection. The word "perfected" here has the idea 'to supply what is lacking in order to see the completeness of it.'

It was also mentioned earlier that God created human beings in order to have us to share His love with. When we love one another with His love, after coming to know Him in salvation, then we are bringing full circle the reason for God giving His love to us in that we not only experience that love ourselves, but we also touch Him Who is invisible in loving with His love. God is known by His love, which is why we read at 1 John 4:8 and again at 1 John 4:16, "God is love." In other words, since God is known by His love, then we pass that reality of God to one another when we love with God's love imparted to us. Let us note here what God further says to us at 1 John 4:7,8, while keeping in mind all that we have just noted above, "[7] Beloved, let us love one another, for love is from God; and everyone who loves is born of God and knows God. [8] The one who does not love does not know God, for God is love." And so, when we love one another as believers, we show that we have been born of God and know God, for love is from God and God Himself is known as really existing by His love.

But that is not all which we should be aware of here. God also reveals another truth at Galatians 5:22,23 that we should note, "[22] But the fruit of the Spirit is love, joy, peace, patience, kindness, goodness, faithfulness, [23] gentleness, self-control; against such things there is no law." It was stated a number of times in the book so far that when we walk with God with no known unconfessed sins in our lives, then He continually imparts His own life for us to live by, which God also refers to as His righteousness in His word, the Bible. And how we can tell that we are being imparted God's life to live by moment by moment, by God The Father through His precious Son by The precious Holy Spirit in our spirit, is due to the fruit of The Spirit being evident in our lives. And please note that the first evidence of God's life being imparted is His love, followed by His joy, then His peace, and so forth. And so for our present purpose here then, we are to note that although God is unseen, His Presence may be felt in us when we walk by His life, with the first sign of that life being His love. In an earlier chapter, I mentioned a certain captain in the Salvation Army being a walking display to me personally of God's love whenever I met him, as just a young believer. But may God find all of us to be such vessels of God's life and His love in these dark last days of the present age!

In reality, there is no last word when it comes to God's love!

CHAPTER SEVENTEEN

/ A last word

In this book, we have looked at the love of God, which is as eternal as God is, which entered into time through God's Son, reaching its height in the death at the cross of His precious Son, Jesus Christ. It is a love that never ceases, is without bounds, and unmeasurable! It is the love that God freely bestows upon every precious soul whom He saves in time, which is never based on merit from anyone, but solely based on the intrinsic love of God, as that which has always existed and always will exist. It is a love that is transformative, so that when one comes into contact with the love of God, one is never the same. It is a love that meets our deepest needs as human beings and satisfies our most pressing yearnings. It is the love that once experienced, we do not want to live without.

God's love is the glue that binds mankind to one another. Let us note one statement which God Himself makes about love in His word at Colossians 3:14, "Beyond all these things put on love, which is the perfect bond of unity." That term, "the perfect bond of unity," literally means 'the uniting bond of perfection.' God's love cannot ever be improved upon. If you have experienced God's love in salvation, will you not this day give Him praise and thanks for it. And if you have not experienced that love that surpasses all understanding, then the chapter included in the Addendum of this book has been included specifically for you!

To God alone be all praise, honor, and glory, with thanksgiving, both now and forevermore! Amen, amen, and amen.

"Jesus said to him, "I am the way, and the truth, and the life; no one comes to the Father but through Me." "

John 14:6

ADDENDUM

/ For those who may not as yet know God

Possibly you have been reading this book and have become aware of not knowing this God Who created us and gave us physical life into this world, and up to now has allowed you to live on earth. However, you do have the desire to know God in a personal way. If this is the case, then this chapter has been written specifically for you. And what God wants you to have in coming to know Him is the peace and joy which comes in knowing that all of your sins committed in your lifetime are forgiven and that you have eternal life with God. And so, your greatest need at the moment is to make peace with God so as to go to Heaven, which is God's eternal home. And so this chapter will help to bring that about by pointing you to God so as to come to faith in Him.

And as we begin, we need to note a most important promise which God makes at Romans 6:23 to all those who do not yet know Him, "For the wages of sin is death, but the free gift of God is eternal life in Christ Jesus our Lord." The good news here is that God offers you eternal life with Him as a free gift, which is to be obtained in His Son, Jesus Christ. What God does not do in this verse from the Bible is tell us how to obtain that eternal life with Him.

Another verse which we can look at where God does let us know how one can obtain that eternal life with Him is noting what God tells us at John 3:16, "For God so loved the world, that He gave His only begotten Son, that whoever believes in Him shall not perish, but have eternal life." Now the added truth which God makes known here is that the eternal life, which He gives to a human being as a free gift, is for those who believe in His Son.

Then the question is: What is it that I am to believe about God's Son, Jesus Christ, which will lead God to give me eternal life with Him forever? And the beauty of God is that He never leaves us guessing, especially when it comes to having a personal relationship with Him, which He desires us to have. Therefore, we should not be surprised when God gives us the answer to our question in what He tells us at 1 Corinthians 15:1-4, "[1] Now I make known to you, brethren, the gospel which I preached to you, which also you received, in which also you stand, [2] by which also you are saved, if you hold fast the word which I preached to you, unless you believed in vain. [3] For I delivered to you as of first importance what I also received, that Christ died for our sins according to the Scriptures, [4] and that He was buried, and that He was raised on the third day according to the Scriptures..." Therefore, "the gospel," which simply means 'good news,' which God wants you to hear and believe in order to "be saved," which simply refers to you coming to know God and have eternal life with Him, is that His Son has already died for you, has already been buried, and has already been raised from the dead again the third day after His death, in order that God would have a basis by which to forgive you of all your sins, which are all against Him, and to freely give you eternal life with Him, for simply believing this message in your heart.

One thing which often prevents a person from believing the gospel at this point is not seeing oneself as a sinner before a Holy God. When we look at ourselves by our own assessment, and especially when we compare ourselves with others around us, we often think of ourselves as being better than others, and so good enough to enter Heaven in our present condition. The problem with this is that it is the product of our own thinking and is not God's assessment of our situation. God's assessment of our situation is as He tells us at Romans 3:10-12,23 in part, "[10] as it is written, "There is none righteous, not even one... [11] there is none who seeks for God [12] all have turned aside... there is none who does good, there is not even one... [23] for all have sinned and fall short of the glory of God..." Quite a different assessment of the human race from that which we as human beings often have of ourselves, is this not? But why would God have such an assessment of the whole human race? For the answer to that question, we need to be aware that God is Creator of all that exists, so that when God created the first man, Adam, at the beginning of time, God created him in innocence,

98

meaning that Adam as first created by God neither knew good nor evil, nor was there any sin anywhere in God's original sinless creation.

However, the day came when God tested Adam with a command, saying to him in the garden of Eden here on earth, which was the perfect environment which God had for him, what we now read at Genesis 2:16,17, "The Lord God commanded the man, saying, "From any tree of the garden you may eat freely; [17] but from the tree of the knowledge of good and evil you shall not eat, for in the day that you eat from it you will surely die." How important to see here that God gave Adam, who although a real person was also representative of the whole human race, the warning of the penalty of death for disobedience to His command.

Unfortunately, the day did come when Adam did partake of the forbidden tree and thereby did sin against God. The moment that happened, Adam not only became a sinner by practice, but also a sinner by nature. One thing my parents had to continually do while under their care was to restrain me from continually going the wrong way, for it seemed that of myself I could not do good, but kept going into sin. The reason this was happening is that from the age of accountability onwards, I had not only become a sinner by practice, but also a sinner by nature. And here the age of accountability needs to be seen as being when as a young child in innocence - which moment is known only by God - one comes to learn the right from the wrong and chooses the wrong, thereby becoming personally accountable to God for one's own sin against Him, since all sin is first of all against Him. And that is why God can say at Romans 3:23 above that "all have sinned and fall short of the glory of God," because God knows that all human beings will go the way of Adam, our representative man, which is also why God can say what He does in regards to the whole of the human race at Romans 5:12, where we read, "Therefore, just as through one man (Adam) sin entered into the world, and death through sin, and so death spread to all men, because all sinned" (from the age of accountability onward).

And so we see that the whole human race is declared by God to not only be sinners by practice and by nature from the age of accountability onwards, but the whole of the human race is now subject to death! In other words, in God's sight the whole of the human race is under the judgment of the penalty of death, due to all being sinners by practice and by nature. You will recall above, in the first verse we quoted from Romans 6:23, God did say there that "the wages of sin is death." And what God means by "death" here is not just loss of physical life, when the physical body we have dies, but also has spiritual death in mind, which is far worse! Spiritual death has its beginning when a separation takes place between a person and God at the moment one becomes a sinner at the age of accountability and ends after the final judgment of time, when God forever casts away from His Presence those who before physical death refused to believe in His Son, Jesus Christ, thereby personally forfeiting the forgiveness of their sins and eternal life with God. And now all such will pay the penalty for their own sins in hell, away from the Presence of God forever.

It is in the midst of such a hopeless situation in which the whole of the human race found itself in that God TOOK THE INITIATIVE and sent His own eternally existing Son into the world, as born of a virgin in the innocence of Adam – so as not to inherit the sinful nature passed on from generation after generation from Adam onwards – so that He might be the acceptable sacrifice offered to God His Father at the cross, there bearing our sins in His body, and there dying the death due our sins! God's Son, Jesus Christ, was then buried and raised from the dead the third day, to ever be alive, for it is through Him, on the basis of what God has done for us through His Son, that God The Father forgives our sins and imparts us eternal life.

Now, by God's grace and His enablement, may you see your need of God's Son to be Your Savior from the penalty due sin, which is death, not only physical, but also spiritual. And by God's grace, may He lead you to believe in His Son, Jesus Christ, and in believing, to receive the forgiveness of your sins and eternal life with Him forever! And based on the truth just shared, the author would now like to ask you a few questions, with the answer being just between yourself and God:

When God says at Romans 3:23, "for all have sinned and fall short of the glory of God," does that include you?

When God says at Romans 5:8, "But God demonstrates His own love toward us, in that while we were yet sinners, Christ died for us," were you included in Christ's death on behalf of sinners?

And when God further says at 1 Peter 3:18 in part, "For Christ also died for sins once for all, the just for the unjust, so that He might bring us to God, having been put to death in the flesh, but made alive in the spirit," were you part of the unjust for whom Christ died?

When God says at Romans 6:23, "For the wages of sin is death, but the free gift of God is eternal life in Christ Jesus our Lord," do you want that eternal life as a free gift from God?

When God says at John 3:16, "For God so loved the world, that He gave His only begotten Son, that whoever believes in Him shall not perish, but have eternal life," do you now believe that Jesus Christ is indeed God's Son in human flesh, Who came from Heaven to this earth to die in your place, so as to save you from ever experiencing the judgment of God leading to an eternal separation from God in hell?

And when God then further says to you at Isaiah 55:6, "Seek the Lord while He may be found; call upon Him while He is near," for His further promise to you here is as we read at Romans 10:9-11,13, "[9] that if you confess with your mouth Jesus as Lord, and believe in your heart that God raised Him from the dead, you will be saved (that is, you will now enter into a personal relationship with God by faith); [10] for with the heart a person believes, resulting in righteousness (that is, in now receiving God's own righteous life to live by), and with the mouth he confesses, resulting in salvation (that is, in now receiving as a free gift the forgiveness of sins and eternal life with God). [11] For the Scripture says, "Whoever believes in Him will not be disappointed..." [13] for "Whoever will call on the name of the Lord will be saved." Will you now call upon God from your heart, telling God in your own words your answer to each question that has just been asked?

The author's prayer for you at this point, as you now call upon God by His grace, is what we read at Romans 15:13, "Now may the God of hope fill you with all joy and peace in believing, so that you will abound in hope by the power of the Holy Spirit."

If there is anyone who desires further spiritual help, please visit my website below:

http://www.servantofmosthigh.com

/ The next book

I am not sure at this time what the title of the next book will be. So it would be best for readers to stay current with one of the author's websites, under "Books," where it will be made known what the title is, if there is another book. My main website is:

http://www.pilgrimpathwaypublications.com

And if you have enjoyed reading this book, or any other of the author's books, please feel free to give me feedback at the above website, and also let family, friends, and co-workers know about this book and other books. The author is not on any social media sites, so he relies on God and readers like you to spread the word. May God bless you for doing so.

Made in the USA
Charleston, SC
06 August 2015